KEYS TO TRANSFORM YOUR LIFE

Three Questions to Using the Key System of Informal Assessments

G. LAMONT DOUGLAS MS, LPC/MHSP

ISBN 979-8-89130-610-3 (paperback)
ISBN 979-8-89130-611-0 (digital)

Christian Faith Publishing
832 Park Avenue
Meadville, PA 16335
www.christianfaithpublishing.com

Printed in the United States of America

FOREWORD

I have had the privilege of being Lamont Douglas's pastor for several years and quickly grew to appreciate his humor, his gentle nature, and his deep desire to help people in distress. And always, it was his evenness, his steadiness, his consistency that caught my attention. No wonder he was drawn to vocation of clinical therapy.

Formally educated at the University of Tennessee, he realized his gift for listening, for "reading" people, and for adapting his clinical skills to their life situation. And over the years, he has refined those skills, working with individuals, families, children, and college students.

We are all busy, and we still feel the effects of COVID-19. Stress is still high. We all want a method, a plan that helps us help others in a healthier and holistic way, and we need that plan to flow out of research and practicality, clinical training, and integrity. We also want a method that is adaptable yet consistently "works" because it has real depth. We want a method that helps our clients make measurable progress.

I was intrigued when Lamont first shared the unassuming outline and questions with me. I tossed out some sample situations—real life struggles and pain. He unpacked the process, the homework, the follow-up sessions; and it all made such sense—authentic, simple, deep, real, accessible to the client, and consistent for the counselor.

This method is the tool I wish I had learned decades ago. It's what I was looking for, and I've been happy to share it with my colleagues and our own staff. With the demanding schedule of work and life, I was immediately drawn to both the simplicity and depth of this approach to therapy. And now, I am honored to recommend it to you.

—Wade Bibb, PhD
Senior Pastor
Central Baptist Church of Bearden
Knoxville, Tennessee

ACKNOWLEDGMENTS

I have so many people to thank who have helped and encouraged me in writing this. I can't possibly mention everyone. First, there is God Almighty, who gave me the inspiration to develop and use the methods that are listed in this book. Thanks to my dear wife, Kristi, who has encouraged and withstood my many moods and the time I have taken from her as I have been involved in this process of writing and the many, many revisions it has taken to publish this. My wife Kristi has been my go-to person to listen to me as I work through my thoughts and put them into organized statements. I have to thank my many friends and colleagues who have helped and encouraged me to share my knowledge and experience. Many thanks go to my special friend and minister, Dr. Wade Bibb, who encouraged me to move forward with writing this book after several conversations. Wade was one of the first, besides myself, to start using these assessments with his work. Many thanks to my daughter, Evie Douglas, for the idea and for making the cover art for this book. Being an author is not something I have thought I would actually do. I have humbly taken on writing this to share my twenty-plus years of experience as a mental health therapist so others can hopefully use these tools and ideas to assist others. I know that God has been the source of wisdom and guidance throughout my career, and the Key System of Informal Assessments has been developed through God's guidance.

CHAPTER 1

Introduction to the Key System of Informal Assessments

The Key System of Informal Assessments helps to unlock the needs, wants, and barriers of individuals and develop measurable and obtainable goals for them to pursue. Most of the tools that mental health professionals use to help people focus mainly on formal assessments and screeners. These formal assessments focus mostly on more specific diagnoses. This is important, yet it does not help the therapist get insight into specific individual goals that the client might have or need. During my practice, I have looked for an assessment that would help people who are struggling with how to get in touch with the core of who they are, where they need to be, and how to reach personal goals. There have not been any formal or informal needs assessments that I have found that achieve this. So, I have developed the Key System of Informal Assessments that I use in my practice that worked and want to share them. These assessments have been developed from my practice of over twenty-five years working with individuals, couples, and families. I have been encouraged by several colleagues and friends in other professions to share my experience and the assessments I have developed and used. In preparation for starting this book, I shared my ideas with other people I knew in other professions, and these individuals shared with me how they liked the concepts and how they used them. The simplicity of the Key System of Informal Assessments is what makes the system so flexible and versatile. The Key System was first developed for use as mental health informal assessment. When the Key System was shared with those who are outside the mental health domain, they found that the simplicity was easy to understand and could help them when they are working with people. This book is designed to be used by both those who are in the mental health field as well as other people who find themselves in informal counseling roles due to their profession. The Key System is designed to be flexible and help start introspection and guide the discussions and interactions with individuals as they work with multiple professionals. This first chapter is designed to explain the overall concept and how the Key System works, and then in later chapters to focus on specific assessments that are designed for various purposes.

The Key System of Informal Assessments is broken down into "Seven Keys."

- *Needs*: What does the individual list as what they need?
- *Wants*: What does the individual list as what they want?
- *Barriers*: What does the individual list as standing in their way?
- *Definition*: Define and clarify the needs, wants, and barriers.

- *Measurable*: Collaborate with the individual to put their needs, wants, and barriers in measurable terms.
- *Time*: Collaborate with the individual on setting realistic timelines to meet the needs and wants and overcome barriers.
- *Positive*: Collaborate with the individual to change barriers into positives that can overcome perceived barriers and have the needs and wants stated in positives.

The instructions for using the Key System are to give just enough instruction to have the individual understand what the purpose is and what they need to do. Being vague helps the client make the assessment their own and start the introspection process. The introspection of the individual is what makes the Key System work. The Key System of Informal Assessments is best used with average and higher intellectual functioning individuals who are at least sixteen years old. Under sixteen years of age, the developmental stage can make these assessments increasingly ineffective. The intelligence level needs to be where the individual can have introspection into their lives and what is going on around them for these assessments to be effective.

The Key System can be used by mental health professionals to help develop and hone treatment plans, measure progress, define other needed goals, and close the therapeutic relationship. The professions outside of mental health mentioned in this book can use the Key System in similar ways. The great advantage of the Key System is that it helps the individual use introspection to see their needs, wants, and what is standing in their way (barriers). Using the Key System of Informal Assessments helps begin the introspection of the individual, which promotes the jump start for the counseling process. For all the professions discussed in this book, the Key System can help identify barriers to realistic and unrealistic expectations and help individuals set goals. Most people seek counseling and the professions mentioned in this book when they are facing transitions in their lives, overwhelmed by circumstances around them, struggling with conflicting roles or expectations, and having difficulty expressing their needs to others.

When using the Key System of Informal Assessments, it is important not to give the individual much instruction. This helps foster the introspection part of these assessments. Introspection is the key to unlocking the individual's perspective of what they *need*, *want*, and *barriers* for themselves. It is recommended that they complete the assessment, then put it aside and come back to it a day or two later. When they complete the assessment, this is the time to work with them on how to make what they list as needs and wants into measurable and obtainable goals.

One of the keys to this system is to help the individual learn how they would measure progress to their listed needs and wants. Focus on wording it in a way that the individual understands. Working with the individual to focus on putting these needs and wants in measurable and obtainable terms can help them to follow their progress. Sometimes their goal is not directly measurable, then work with them to find tangible goals that can be used to measure progress toward goals. A good example of this is an individual who writes, "A good relationship with my spouse." This is a good goal but difficult to put into measurable terms. Some tangents to this could be to reduce conflicts to one time a month with the spouse, spend quality time with a spouse two times a week, or have at least two thirty-minute conversations with the spouse a week. After working on defining the responses in measurable terms then work on setting a reasonable time line for these goals that is obtainable. Help them understand that before Hades freezes over is not a timeline. Understanding that having a timeline is not written in stone either. Timelines can and should be flexible. For instance, an individual wants to buy a new car but has an unexpected medical bill that affects the money set aside for getting a new car. They then might need to readjust the timeline for the new car.

What the individual lists as needs helps the counselor get insight into their priorities and goals, or lack of them. How well are the needs defined? Vague or simple goals can indicate other struggles that are going on. For instance, if there is a history of significant trauma, the individual can be functioning in a default crisis mode that affects this process. Also, severe depression or very low self-concept can affect this as well, and these individuals have difficulty in listing needs or wants. They do not have difficulty in listing what is standing in their way. If the individual is not able to list any or very few needs, then working with them on broader short-term goals can be a starting point. Of course, the lack of short- or long-term goals can indicate depression, which needs to be explored further. Another sign of depression or trauma can be the listing of very basic needs like food, shelter, etc. This can be correlated to *Maslow's*[1] hierarchy of needs and can indicate the individual is functioning in a crisis mode.

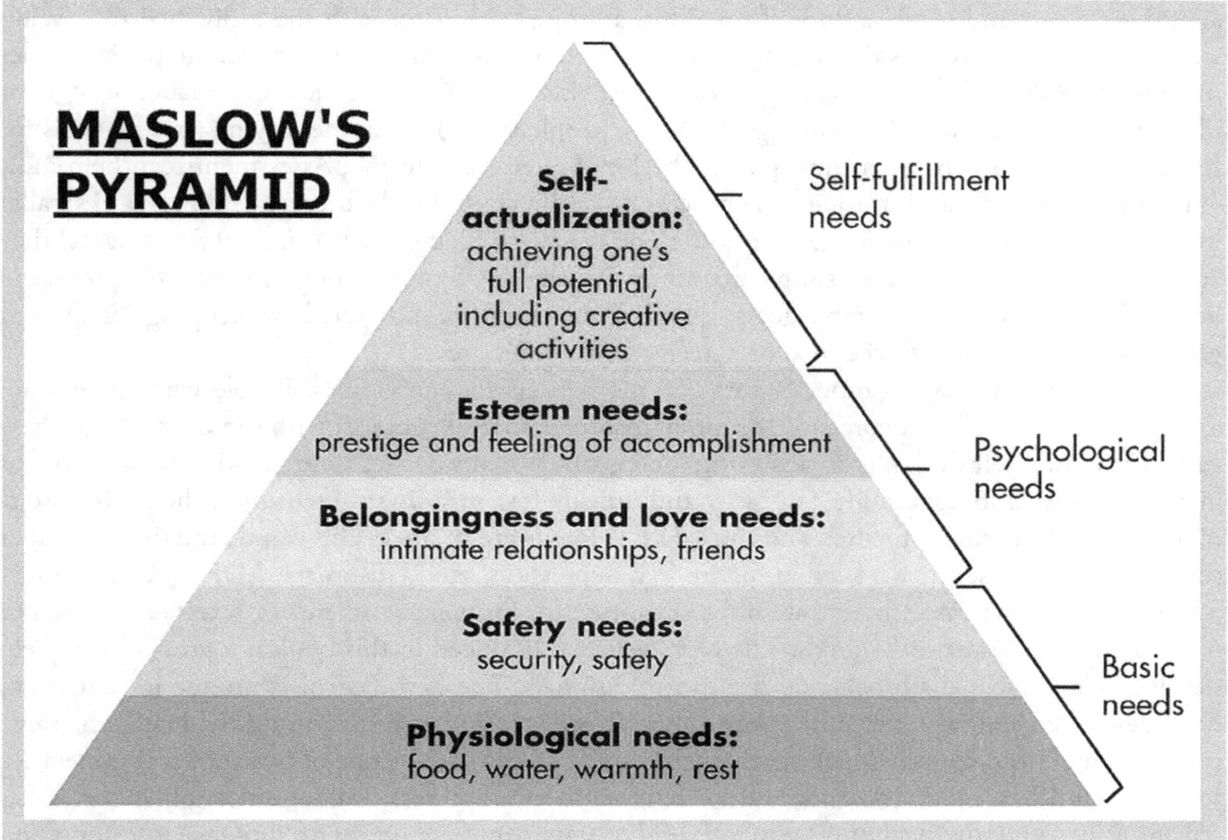

---

[1] Abraham Maslow, ""A Theory of Human Motivation,"" *Psychological Review* (1943).

Maslow proposed that individuals have different needs depending on where they are on his needs. When individuals respond with very basic needs that are on the bottom two levels of the Needs Pyramid, it can mean they are not secure with housing, food, warmth or rest, security, or safety. If this is the case, then any higher needs or wants are not realistic to them. Individuals with Post-traumatic Stress Disorder often feel stuck in this and worry about these basic needs, especially safety, even when they are in a position where these needs are met. The ideal for mental health is for individuals to reach the top of the pyramid and remain there. Very few individuals can reach this, and even fewer can remain at the top for the long term. The Key System of Informal Assessments can help the user to identify where an individual sees themselves on the needs pyramid, and then the clarification questions can help to set goals to be able to move up the pyramid. Users who are not mental health professionals might need to refer individuals who are stuck and remain stuck on the bottom levels of the needs pyramid to have more formal assessments and treatment. For mental health professionals, being stuck or remaining stuck could indicate a higher level of care might be needed for the individual to get the help they need.

These Key Systems can help the user detect realistic and unrealistic thinking. When working on making the needs and wants measurable, this is time to work with the individual on how obtainable these needs and wants are for them. This is the time to work with the individual to develop steps to obtain the needs/wants and break these down, where progress can be measurable in smaller increments. Asking, "How could you measure this?" is a start in helping the individual to break their ideas down into measurable smaller goals. Many people struggle with identifying specific goals for themselves and how to reach these goals. The Key System of Informal Assessments can help individuals identify goals and, through the process of clarification, break these goals down into smaller increments that can be measured. People often do not reach their goals because they do not feel they are making progress. The three simple questions that the Key System is built on starts the process to help individuals make measurable goals. It is very important for individuals to feel progress and not give up due to feeling overwhelmed or perceived lack of progress.

There are times when other factors become barriers for individuals. People who suffer from anxiety, attention deficit, depression, or mood disorders struggle not just with these issues, but these can compound their difficulty in achieving their goals. When a person is not making progress or has given up on reaching goals, life can easily and quickly lose meaning. Oftentimes, the needs assessments can indicate more focused and formal assessments are needed. This can be the time for other screeners/formal assessments such as for anxiety, depression, mood disorders, ADHD, etc. The Key Systems of Informal Assessments are not a substitute for formal assessments or screeners focused or to be used to diagnose individuals. The Key System introduced in this book is a great tool to help develop treatment plans for mental health professionals. The Key System is unique in that is has been developed so that other professions can use the same processes to help individuals. The same process is used to help individuals reach goals specific to the users' scope of practice. It is imperative to understand when individuals need to be referred to other professionals and possibly higher levels of care. When an individual puts better off dead or statements like others need to take over for them, then it is time to consider if a mental health crisis consult is necessary. When there are statements of needing to or wanting to harm others, this is also a time for a mental health crisis consult and consider the duty to warn specific targets and authorities about identified threats. An individual who feels that their needs cannot be met can also need further clarification to know if a crisis consult is needed. When individuals feel they cannot get their needs met, they can become a danger to themselves or to others. A goal of these assessments is to help individuals understand that reasonable goals can be reached and life has a purpose.

The concrete-thinking individual will tend to have more difficulty with the lack of specific instructions with these assessments. Working with individuals who struggle with abstract thinking can sometimes be a challenge. Using these assessment tools can help the concrete thinker to work on acceptance of flexibility, taking the *needs* and *wants* that are listed and working with the individual on making these flexible. When asking how to break their needs/wants into steps, measurable is a time to help them build flexibility into the goals. Have the individual talk about various options at each step and not let changes or setbacks deviate them from their goals. When there is a person who is a very concrete, black-or-white thinker, this can be detected by the lack of flexibility or being able to break down these needs/wants into steps or developing a flexible timeframe for these. The concrete thinker will often give a lot of details, and these seem very rigid and inflexible. When working with this thinking, work on having less details and more flexibility.

The extreme abstract thinker will struggle with specific needs/wants and writes things that are vague and very hard to define in measurable terms. The abstract thinker tends to get lost in the "big picture" and often can give up or feel goals are unreachable or hopeless due to not seeing or feeling progress. The process can start to help individuals make measurable goals that can help them know the progress and go from the strictly big picture to steps that help them.

The clarification process is another key starting point for the Key System Assessments. When an individual lists a need or want, ask, "What does that mean to you?" There are many terms and concepts that have "official" definitions. Most people have a personal definition for certain terms; for example, family or friends has a dictionary definition. When asked, most individuals will give a personal definition based on their experiences and expectations. Once the individual clarifies their personal definition, then start to ask, "How can we measure progress toward this?" Work with them on how they can break these down into smaller goals and be able to see progress.

The most important key to the Key System of Informal Assessments is the question of what is standing in your way. This question is asked in several different ways depending on the specific assessment used. When individuals start to identify what is standing in their way, they are identifying barriers they feel are keeping them from reaching goals. Start asking the individual to clarify what is standing in their way by asking, "Why is this standing in your way?" Then, ask them what they can do to start overcoming the barriers. The next step is to work with the individual to state how to overcome barriers in measurable terms. In doing this, the user is working with the individual to change barriers into a positive and understanding how to work on change that can help them in the long term.

To give an example, I had an individual say that for the Intake Needs Assessment, they need "to have better control of my emotions." I read this and asked them to clarify what specifically they mean by that. They stated that they have emotional outbursts and worked with them to clarify further what specifically they mean by outbursts. The individual reported that they got angry and started yelling at family members when they get frustrated. Asking the individual how they would put this in measurable terms, like, "How would you know if you are making progress with controlling your anger?" This allows them to think through how they can know steps to getting this need met, like getting a baseline for anger outbursts and then reducing these outbursts systematically. The next step is to have the individual set timelines to accomplish these reductions, helping them to have a realistic timeline for controlling their anger. If they report they are having about ten outbursts a week, then stopping these completely by two weeks is most likely very unrealistic. Working with the individual to have more realistic steps to achieving the goal of few to no outbursts over a longer period of time with steps to get there is a more realistic and obtainable goal. Worked with this individual on setting a goal of reducing outbursts from over ten to seven a week by two weeks and then reducing the outbursts by two a week every two weeks. This is a much more reasonable timeline and allows the individual to learn anger control and how to apply these.

There was an individual who stated they needed "more motivation and be more positive." The question to ask is, can these be linked? Ask the individual what their definition of motivation is. Then work on them, stating this in measurable terms. How do you measure positivity? A way to put this in measurable terms would be to monitor how many times a week the individual has been engaged in enjoyable activities and how many times a week they feel down and depressed. Once a baseline is established, then setting goals to increase these enjoyable activities in increments that are realistic. Another way to measure positivity is to monitor moods using a scale and, after getting a baseline, set goals for increasing positive and decreasing negative moods.

There was one individual who listed "lack of wisdom" as a barrier that was standing in their way. The first question should be how they define wise. Then work on turning this into a positive by helping the individual. They can start working toward the goal of gaining wisdom. This could be as simple as thinking through responses before speaking or developing a system of self-education.

The idea is to have the individual write out these responses between sessions or meetings. There are times when these assessments can be used in a session or meeting. Using the assessment to write out their responses or having the user write down the individual's responses can also be an effective way to use the Key System Assessments. Some of the assessments can be used as talking points, and using the clarification questions can still help the user get the individual to use the introspection to start the process. The assessments that can most easily be used verbally are the dental- and veterinarian-focused assessments.

The purchaser of this book is authorized to copy and use the Key System of Informal Assessments in this book that are appropriate as often as needed.

CHAPTER 2

The Key System Mental Health Assessments

Individual Assessments

This chapter focuses on the Key System Assessments that are used for individuals. These informal assessments can be great to assist in starting and developing the therapeutic relationship. Since these assessments are completed from the individual's perspective, this can help the user connect with the individual without potential biases of the user interfering. Using these assessments with individuals helps to develop therapeutic goals. Getting input from the assessments assists the user in understanding the individual's perspectives.

The assessments that are used for individuals are the intake, career, educational, parental, relationship-focused, and reassessment. When first meeting an individual, I give them the intake assessment. The individual is then asked to complete this for the next session. If they start to ask for more information, then I tell them that it is their assessment, and giving them more direction affects the usefulness of the assessment. The assessment asks them to list their needs, wants, and what is standing in their way. The only instruction given to the individuals is to complete this before the next session and not to rush the exercise. They are encouraged to work on this and set it aside and come back to it a couple of times and add or change things around as needed.

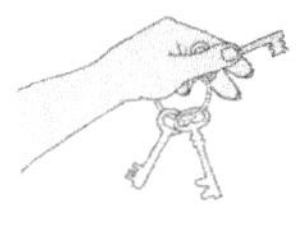

Intake Assessment

What do you need?	What do you want?	What is standing in your way?

When the individual brings the assessment back, then start with the needs and ask them how they define what they have listed. This is the first Key to processing the individual responses. The next Key is to work with the individual so they can measure progress for their needs/wants. Then work on a reasonable timeline for the progress toward the needs helps the individual develop needs into goals. This is also the process for the wants that are listed. This assessment works best if it is individual-led and the user is just guiding them with how to clarify and focus on the needs and wants.

Now to the column "What is Standing in Your Way," this is what makes the Key System of Informal Assessments unique. This is a way to ask the individual to list what they think are barriers to what they need or want. Go through each listed response and work to clarify how to change each of the barriers listed into positives that they can work on to overcome the listed barriers. Then ask questions like "how can you start to overcome this?." The last "Key" is to collaborate with the individual on what they can do to overcome listed barriers and make these measurable. The last step is to have them break down the ways to overcome the barriers into smaller steps with realistic timelines. The Key System of Informal Assessments is a great starting point for working with individuals to clarify their overall goals to better themselves.

The Educational Assessment is used for individuals who are either in or are planning on going to school (high school or any form of higher education). Work with them on the understanding that this focus is on what they need and want from their education as well as what is standing in their way.

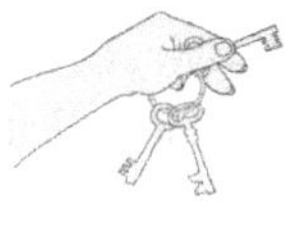

Educational Needs Assessment

What do you need from your education?	What do you want from your education?	What is standing in the way of your education?

Using the same Keys as used in the intake assessment. The first Key is to work with the individual to clearly define what they need/want from their education and educational process. Ask the individual what the purpose of education is for them. Individuals can have unrealistic expectations for their education. There are individuals who expect to get their degree and have a high-paying career job right after graduation. Unfortunately, there are a few majors that might happen, but a large number of individuals will end up in jobs that do not meet their expectations. This assessment can help the individual understand realistic goals for their education and options after graduation. The next Key is to have them state these needs/wants in measurable terms and reasonable time frames. This is a great time to work with the expectations the individual has and if these meet the current and near-future job markets. When working with timelines, it is important to stress flexibility. A lot of people have taken on too much in one semester to be able to graduate by an arbitrary time frame. Use the clarification questions to assist the individual process and further use introspection. This can be a great time to assist the individual in understanding the time and monetary investment of higher education and the potential future for this. The last Key is to work through what the individual lists as barriers they identify as standing in their way. This last Key is used to reframe the barriers into positives, and now they can overcome the barriers. This is a good time to help the individual know how to find resources to help overcome these perceived barriers. The Key System of Informal Assessments is designed to help people set realistic goals for their educational experience and clarify their expectations.

With people changing jobs and careers more often now, the career assessment is a good tool to assist individuals in evaluating where they are and where they want to go with their careers. The first question is to ask the individual to think about either the career/job they have now or the career/job they want to get when the assessment is given to the individual. If a person has not been in the workforce or is returning to the workforce, this can be a good start to help the individual to narrow down their search.

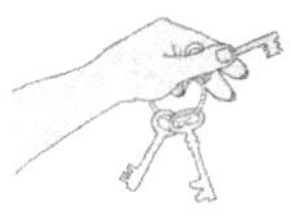

Career Assessment

What do you need in a job/career?	What do you want from a job/career?	What are things that you would not tolerate in a job/career?

The first Key is to work through the individual's needs and wants. Using the clarification questions, work with the individual to clearly define their needs. The next Key is to collaborate with the individual to make the needs/wants measurable where they can know the progress. This helps the individual to understand if their needs and wants are obtainable quickly or will take time, training, or further education to achieve. The next Key is to collaborate with them on further defining their responses to things that they cannot tolerate at a career/job and why. This Key is different from the other assessments. The Key here is to identify what they are not able to tolerate and how they can avoid these situations. Clarification questions like "How do you keep from being in this situation?" or "How do you avoid this in a career/job?" can help them evaluate employment environments and situations. When working with a person who is in a career/job, this assessment can help them to evaluate their current work environment and be able to work toward change in themselves or change in the workplace. When working with an individual who is working on changing jobs or careers, this assessment can help them as they are seeking employment. The responses they give can help them as they research careers/jobs and career/job postings to find one that they can give them the fulfillment they are seeking. These tools can also help people to have questions ready to ask when they go into the interview process.

From my experience, there are not many assessments that mental health case managers can use. The Key System of Informal Assessments can help case managers develop treatment goals and realistic expectations from case management. The first Key starts with the questions, "What do you need, and what do you want from case management services?" Asking clarification questions like what do you know about case management services?

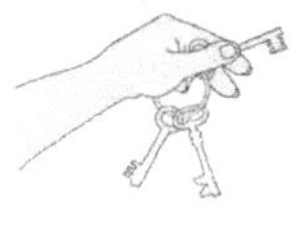

Case Management Assessment

What do you need from case management?	What do you want from case management?	What are things that keep you from being involved in case management?

When beginning to work with an individual who has not been involved in case management before, this can be a great way to have them understand realistic expectations. This assessment is a great way to introduce them to what case management can assist them and the limitations of case management. The first Key is to have the individual define the needs/wants listed. Use clarification questions like, "What does that mean?", "Please tell me more about that," or "Please explain that to me." The next Key is to focus on the individual developing measurable outcomes and goals through a clarification question like, How would that be measured? Work with the individual on understanding realistic and unrealistic goals and expectations for case management. This tool can also be used as needs change due to either changes in circumstances or progress. The next Key focuses on what is keeping you from being involved in case management services, collaborating with the individual on overcoming their obstacles to being involved in case management. The individual might need assistance to define ways that identified barriers can be reframed into positives. This assessment can be read to the individual and used at a meeting if necessary. Often, individuals who need case management services have other obstacles that can affect their introspection and might need some assistance to work with this assessment.

The Reassessing Needs Assessment is specifically designed to help the individual understand progress and continued needs/wants that have not been met and need continued focus. The first question is different. It asks "what needs and wants have been met." This helps the individual think about the progress they have made. This is Key for this assessment since individuals can get lost in day-to-day events, and it becomes easy to overlook the progress they are making. The next Key is the question, "What needs or wants have not been met?"

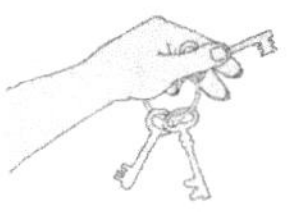

Reassessing Needs

What needs and needs and wants have been met?	What needs or wants have not been met?	What continues to stand in your way?

This Key gives the individual an idea about what they need to continue to work on. Use the clarification questions to help the individual state their continued needs in measurable and obtainable goals like the other assessments. Another Key to using this assessment is to help the individual understand if they have the means to be able to work toward these goals on their own or continue to need assistance in reaching their goals. The last Key question on the reassessment is, "What continues to stand in your way?" Working with the individual on how they can restate what is standing in their way in a way that they can overcome these barriers. This is a great opportunity to gauge if the individual has the means to work on barriers on their own or continues to need assistance. This can also be used as a closing assessment if the individual has progressed to the point they can continue without assistance. When the individual can identify their needs and wants in realistic and measurable terms and can develop their own ways to reach these goals, then this can be a good time to conclude the counseling or case management relationship.

CHAPTER 3

Individual Relationships

This chapter covers informal assessments that are focused on interpersonal relationships. These can be used in two different ways. The first is where an individual is assessing their own interpersonal relationships such as family, friendship, parenting, and romantic. This can be a great start to help individuals understand their own goals and also help to identify issues they might have, like how to set appropriate boundaries or improve their ability to communicate. The second way these assessments can be used is with couples, families, or friendship groups. This chapter focuses on using the assessments with individuals.

The romantic relationship assessment is slightly different than the Intake and Educational Assessments in that it can used with individuals and with couples. How to use this assessment with couples is covered in the chapter for couples and families. In this chapter, the focus will be on how this assessment is used for the individual.

Romantic Relationship Assessment

What do you need in a romantic relationship?	What do you want in a romantic relationship?	What are deal-breakers in a romantic relationship?

The first Key starts with the questions, What do you need, and what do you want from a romantic relationship? These are helpful in setting personal standards for the individual as they are searching for a romantic relationship or evaluating a romantic relationship they are in. When using this assessment, it is important to have the individual focus on all experiences with past romantic relationships as well as future potential romantic relationships. The first Key is to ask the individual to clearly define their responses. The next Key is to state the responses in measurable terms. This can be more work than the other assessments in that most of the responses can be much more abstract. For example, an individual listed they needed respect from their partner. When asked for examples of when they felt they were respected, then this can be the starting point to get specific ideas that can be measured. The next step is to define these responses in a way that can be measurable. Now if the individual is not in a romantic relationship, then a timeline is not needed. When an individual is in a romantic relationship, when they complete this informal assessment, then a reasonable time frame of getting these needs/wants met is important if they are not being met. This is also a good time to help an individual understand that expecting all their needs/wants to be fulfilled by their romantic partner may not be not realistic. It is important for the individual to understand that it is normal to have some needs met appropriately outside of the romantic relationship. As with the other assessments, collaborating with the individual to be able to state the needs/wants is to define these responses in a way that can be measurable so they can know the progress.

The difference with this assessment is the last column that asks, "What are deal-breakers?" This is asking for what the individual cannot tolerate in a relationship. This is a very important key to this assessment. This Key helps the individual understand what specific things or characteristics that would ruin a relationship for them. The great use of this assessment is to help individuals make a measuring stick for themselves. This measuring stick can be used to have the individual understand who reaches or exceeds these expectations they have. This is also a great time to have them evaluate if anyone can measure up to the measuring stick. Does the individual have unrealistic expectations that no one can live up to? This is an opportunity to work with the individual on developing realistic expectations for a romantic partner.

The friendship assessment is an important assessment to help individuals assess past, current, or future friendship relationships. The first Key is to have the individual give their personal definition of friendship. Then start to collaborate with the individual on what they need and want from friendships. Work on how they can define these is to define these responses in a way that can be measurable.

Friendship Assessment

What do you need in a friendship?	What do you want in a friendship?	What are deal-breakers in a friendship?

The Key System of Informal Assessments

If the individual has little to no support system in place, this is a great starting point for them to look at and think about how to start to reach out to others. This Key can help people who have social anxiety. This Key can be a great tool to help when individuals have issues with appropriate boundaries. This can open up the discussion about how to establish healthy boundaries. The next Key is to have the individual define what are deal-breakers for friendships. The next Key is to collaborate with the individual on understanding if the barriers of the deal-breakers are realistic or unrealistic. This assessment can help the individual to develop a "measuring stick" to establish if others are able to measure up to their standards. When a person has a measuring stick, this can help them to feel safer in putting themselves out there.

It is important to be aware that other people can have an influence on the individual's perception of the friendship and be careful to help identify where these needs, wants, and barriers are coming from. Past experiences tend to influence an individual's present relationships. When there are traumas, this can affect an individual's choices and how they list needs, wants, and barriers to friendships. This assessment can open up the discussion of past events that still affect them and start how they can start work on changing these barriers into positives and help them understand how to develop healthy friendships.

The parenting assessment is a tool to help individuals assess the parent-child relationship. This can be used both individually and for couples. In this chapter, the focus will be on how to assess a parenting relationship with individuals who are in a parenting role and their children. This assessment can be used for individuals in parenting roles with children of all ages. One way to use this assessment with individuals who have adult children is to evaluate which parent-child relationships need improvement, in their opinion. When completing this assessment, have the individual focus on the parent-child relationship they feel needs improvement as they complete the assessment. Often, parents can get stuck on past issues and events that affect their current relationship with their adult child, and this assessment can help to identify these past issues. When working with individuals who have younger children and teens, this assessment can assist the user to collaborate with the individual on effective parenting strategies that use the individual's strengths. It can be difficult to enforce effective boundaries with children, and this assessment can be a great starting point to assist the individual in establishing effective parenting strategies.

The first Key is to have the individual give an overall personal definition of an effective parent and then specifically to an individual child. Start by clarifying what the individual feels that they think it is to be a great parent. Then collaborating with the individual on what they think it is to be a great parent to a specific child. This is a great time to work on them, understanding the examples of parenting that they had when they grew up, and what they want to duplicate and what they do not. The next Key is to collaborate with the individual to state what they need to be an effective parent in a way that is measurable and obtainable. Once this has been done, then the Key to defining what they want from the parenting relationship is used. This is a great way to get insight into possible unrealistic expectations the individual might have. There have been individuals who have listed they wanted their children to be their best friends. This is the time to work with this individual on the understanding that being a best friend with their child is often contradictory to setting boundaries and rules for their child. The next Key is to have the individual define these terms into measurable ideas related to the parenting relationship.

With so many coparenting situations, the needs and wants can easily be affected by the relationship with the coparent rather than the child. This assessment can help to identify if this is a factor in the parent-child relationship. If the parenting relationship is being affected by the relationship with the coparent, then this can be addressed and, subsequently, improve the individual parent-child relationship.

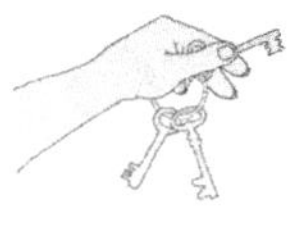

Parenting Assessment

What do you need to help you be a great parent?	What do you want from your parenting relationship?	What stands in your way from being a great parent?

The last Key is to focus on what the individual believes is standing in the way of being an effective parent. When these barriers have been identified they work to focus on positive, measurable ways, they can work to overcome these barriers. This last Key of identifying barriers also helps the individual identify areas they need help with.

Work on how these can be stated in measurable terms. This can be as simple as affordable child-care and as complex as understanding how they need to follow through with disciplinary actions. The next question helps us understand how they see and want the child-parent relationship to be. Ask the individual to clarify if there are conflicting roles and then how this can be put into measurable terms so they can know how they are making progress. The Key to this assessment is the question of what is standing in your way of being a great parent. Work with the individual on changing these into positives and how they can then measure progress in overcoming what they feel are weaknesses.

The parenting assessment can be a great place to understand that the individual's experience growing up can have a direct influence on their effectiveness in a parenting role. Using the Key of clarification questions that focus on where their needs and wants are rooted can help. If the past experiences of the individual are negatively affecting their parenting attitudes or strategies, then this a good place to start a therapeutic focus.

The Family Relationship Needs Assessments are used with individuals to help them assess family relationships. This can be focused on either family, friendships, or romantic relationships. The flexibility of these assessments is very helpful. When you have an individual who is struggling with relationships, these assessments can help them to figure out what they can do to improve or to know which relationships are toxic for them.

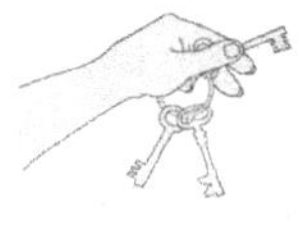

Family Relationship Assessment

What do you need from family relationships?	What do you want from family relationships?	What are things that stand in your way of family relationships?

There are three different relationship assessments: family, friendships, and romantic. When using the Family Relationship Needs Assessment, it is important to have the individual focus on what the people they define as family. This assessment can help individuals start to identify what they need from their families. For example, an individual stated that family means related by blood and always has your back. Then when asked who they felt fit that definition, the individual started to say that most of their biological family did not fit that definition. When asking for further clarification, the individual stated there are people who have their back and are not biological family. Then using the assessment, the individual began to think in broader terms in their definition of family. They realized that they have friends who are like family members and expanded their definition of family.

CHAPTER 4

Couples and Family Assessments

This chapter focuses on the Key Assessments used with couples and families. This allows groups to understand each other's perspectives. The focus is on positives and starting the individuals to focus on similarities. When working with couples, the needs assessments that are most used are the romantic relationship, parenting, financial, and retirement assessments. When working with a couple or larger group, these assessments start with the individuals completing the assessment before a session. During the session, the user then compares the responses and starts with those that are similar. When working with responses that are clearly different, this is an opportunity to engage not only the individual and have the other participants to discuss options as well.

When starting to work with a couple that are having issues with their relationship, start with each individual completing a relationship assessment. After each individual completes the assessment, then have the couple bring these to the next session.

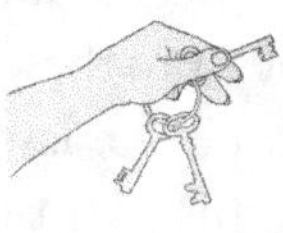

Romantic Relationship Assessment

What do you need in a romantic relationship?	What do you want in a romantic relationship?	What are deal-breakers in a romantic relationship?

The first Key is to find where there are similarities in the responses they list. Sometimes, these are in various columns, and this is where to start to ask clarification questions to both individuals on what they have listed. A Key here is to ask for personal definitions of what they have listed. The next Key is a collaboration with each individual on clarification of the needs listed. It is best to start by asking the partner how the needs and wants can be measured. If the partner is not able to state how the needs can be measured, then collaborate with the individual to help their partner understand how to measure these needs and break these into smaller goals. The potentially tricky part of this assessment can be the last column, where they list things that will not tolerated. Keeping a positive focus is key with this part of the assessment. Collaborate with the couple on ways to overcome barriers that are stated. Help them to identify positive and measurable ways these barriers can be overcome.

When working with the Key of clarifying wants/needs, it is important to stress that there are needs/wants that might have to be appropriately met outside of the romantic relationship. Many individuals get into a relationship and believe that the romantic relationship will fulfill all of their needs and wants. This thinking oftentimes creates a great deal of pressure on the romantic relationship. This is a great time to work with the couple on understanding what needs and wants their partner can provide and understand how to get fulfillment on the other needs/wants appropriately.

Oftentimes, couples come into therapy due to differences in parenting styles. The Keys for the Parenting Assessment are different from the other assessments. The Keys used asks, "What do you need to be an effective parent?" What do you want to help you be a more effective parent?" and lastly, "What is standing in your way to being an effective parent?"

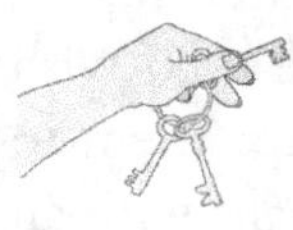

Parenting Assessment

What do you need to help you be a great parent?	What do you want from your parenting relationship?	What stands in your way from being a great parent?

When working with couples, asking them to complete this individually and then both bring this back to the office is ideal. Start by looking for similarities between the Parenting Assessments and work on these first. Like the relationship assessment, then start to alternate between the individual's responses with the clarification process. It is important to help the parents strive for unity and use this to understand individual strengths and potential weaknesses when it comes to parenting.

When working with families, the flexibility of family assessment is that it can be used with multiple family members. The assessment is given to each family member and asked for them to independently complete the assessment. The important Key to using the family assessment with all the family members is that each family member now has a voice. This assessment allows each family member to identify what they feel they needs, wants, and barriers to the family relationships. The first Key is to have each individual give their personal definition of what family means to them. The next Key in using the family assessment is to compare what they consider as the needs/wants of a family relationship. First, start with similarities that are common and collaborate with the individuals to define what they list as needs/wants in measurable terms. The next Key is to collaborate with family members on clarifying the measurable needs/wants with realistic timelines. The next Key is to focus on the differences that individuals list and collaborate with them to clarify these needs in measurable terms.

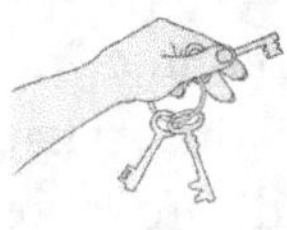

Family Relationship Assessment

What do you need from family relationships?	What do you want from family relationships?	What is standing in your way of family relationships?

The last Key of this assessment is asking, "What is standing in your way of family relationships?" Start with similarities and focus on how to change these into positives to overcome the barriers listed. Then collaborate with the family members on defining these in measurable ways so they can overcome the barriers each family member has. Next, collaborate with individuals on the different responses listed in the same manner. There can be some individual issues that are listed that are better addressed in individual sessions rather than family sessions. Examples of this can be like "no one in the family likes me," "don't fit in with this family," or "afraid to tell anyone in my family what I think or feel." These or other statements that are more focused on themselves usually indicate there are individual issues that need to be addressed before the family issues can be effectively overcome.

There is an old adage that couples often fight over money and who controls the money. This is where the Financial Assessment can help a couple to sort out their financial goals and focus. Give this to each individual and have them complete the assessment separately. When they come together, then collect these and compare the responses listed to identify the similarities and the differences.

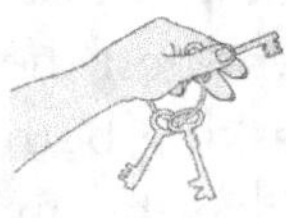

Financial Assessment

What do you need from your financial resources?	What do you want from your financial resources?	What is standing in the way of reaching your financial goals?

Similarly to the other couples' assessments, the first Key is to identify common themes or similarities in their needs /wants. The next Key used is to ask each individual their individual definition of financial stability and success. Financial stability and financial success can have some similarities, yet the differences in these are the Key to collaborating with the couple on setting financial goals. The next Key is to start to collaborate on similar responses to the needs/wants with the clarification questioning and focus on stating these in measurable terms. The next Key is to work on the needs/wants responses that are different and alternating between the individuals and asking both to participate in the clarification process. The next Key is to collaborate with them to identify any common themes that they list as barriers and start to change these into positives they can work on in measurable terms. The next Key is to collaborate with each individual on barriers listed that are different from their partner. Asking the partner how these can be stated in positive ways to overcome the barriers helps the couple to learn better communication.

Working with couples that are in the life stage where they are starting to think about putting resources back for retirement or nearing retirement ages can be a challenge. The Retirement Assessment works great for the couple to set both individual goals and goals for them as a couple. Giving each individual this assessment and asking them to complete the assessments independently is a must to get each individual's perspective. The first Key here is identifying common themes for the needs/wants and making these measurable.

Retirement Assessment

What do you need when you retire?	What do you want from retirement?	What is keeping you from retirement?

The next Key of clarification should also include questions about inheritance. This is a great time to ask the couple about their ideas on the division of assets after death. This is often a contentious subject with couples, especially couples that are remarried and part of a blended family. A lot of couples might briefly discuss these or assume they are in agreement on this when they are not. Getting the couple to understand what they would want for each other and family members after death is an important subject to discuss. Using the clarification questions can identify the common themes the couple has. This helps to get both partners to be engaged in the process. It is important to alternate between the individuals to further define their needs/wants in measurable terms. The next Key is to alternate between the individuals to have them identify what they see as barriers when they answer what is standing in their way. Then refocus the responses for "What is keeping you from retirement?" into positives that can be measured and obtained.

CHAPTER 5

Foster Care and Adoption

Individuals who are interested in becoming foster parents or adopting children have very loving hearts. There are many reasons people choose to foster or adopt children. The Key System can assist those who are working with new or current foster or adoptive parents. Often, individuals who want to become foster parents can have unrealistic expectations about being foster parents. This assessment is used in two different ways. The Foster Care and Adoption assessments are focused on individuals, couples, and families who are wanting to foster or adopt children. The emphasis is assisting people with understanding their personal goals and realistic and unrealistic expectations they might have. Individuals can have all kinds of motivations to be a foster or adoptive parent. These assessments can help users identify potential issues that can interfere with the foster or adoptive process.

The first Key is to have an individual complete the foster care assessment. Then ask them to define what their responses are to the first key question of what they need to be an effective foster parent. A clarification question that can be used is to ask, "Why is this important to you?" This is where the user can assist the individual with understanding realistic and unrealistic needs that they have. The next Key is to ask how these responses can be measured to know progress.

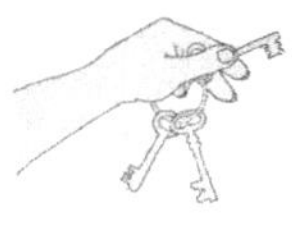

Foster Care Needs Assessment

What do you need to be an effective foster parent?	What do you want in a foster care relationship?	What is keeping you from being a foster parent?

The next Key is to work with the second question of, "What do you want in a foster care relationship?" This question focuses on what motivates the individual to be a foster parent. This Key is designed to help individuals define their responses in a way that can be measurable. This is also a time to help the individual understand what wants might be unrealistic and help them to address these. Next is to assist the individual with what they feel is keeping them from being a foster parent. The last Key is to work with the individual to identify positives that will counter their perceived barriers. These assessments help with the introspection of the individual to understand their personal goals related to being foster parents.

The other way to use this assessment is to have each foster parent complete this assessment individually. The first Key here is to compare the responses of the couple and start with the similarities. The next step is to use the clarification questions to help them define their responses more specifically. Have the couple define these responses in a way that can be measurable. The next step is to work on the responses that are not similar on each assessment. Have the couple work together to clarify these responses. The next Key is to define these responses in a way that can be measurable. When the couple identifies barriers, this is a time to work with the couple on how they can overcome the listed barriers to being foster parents.

Those who adopt children are very special. It is important that prospective adoptive parents have an understanding of their motivations and expectations when it comes to adopting. The Adoption Needs Assessment is a great tool for having the adoptive parent or couple to start the introspection process. The first Key is to work with the individual who is thinking about adopting a child on defining their responses. Start by asking them to further define their responses to "What do you need to be a good adoptive parent?" Then continue with the clarification questions like, "How do you define a good adoptive parent?" The next set of clarification questions uses the next Key of measurably. These questions should focus on how the individual would measure being a good adoptive parent. As with all these assessments, the user should work with the individual on any possible unrealistic expectations that they might express during this process. The next Key of setting timelines for changes that the individual feels are needed to meet the defined goals is important.

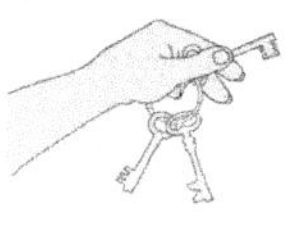

Adoption Needs Assessment

What do you need to be a good adoptive parent?	What do you want in an adoptive relationship?	What could keep you from adopting?

The next Key is to work through what the individual wants from the adoptive relationship. This question can get to the motivations an individual has to adopt. This is a great time to work through any unrealistic motivations that the individual has about adopting a child. Next, use the Key to help define and clarify what the individual wants from the adoptive relationship.

The last Key is to work through what the individual feels are barriers to being an adoptive parent. Take the responses to "What would keep you from being an adoptive parent," and use the Key of positives to assist the individual in developing ways to overcome perceived barriers. Using clarification questions like, "How can we define a positive way to overcome this?" or "What is a resource that can be used to overcome this?"

When working with a couple that is looking to adopt, this assessment can help the couple to be on the same page with each other. After the individuals have completed the Adoption Needs Assessment, the user should compare the responses. First, start with similar responses and help them to further define these in ways that can be measured. The most effective way to accomplish the definitions is to alternate between the individual's responses. This can keep the individuals from thinking that their ideas are not as important or being singled out. The next step is to focus on the responses that are distinctly different and have the other individual assist in defining these responses in measurable ways. Have the individuals and couple view barriers as opportunities for growth, and there are ways to overcome barriers they perceive.

CHAPTER 6

The Key System for Spiritual Assessments

The spiritual assessments are designed for ministers and mental health professionals to use. There are not a lot of assessments for ministers to use as they counsel individuals. These assessments were designed with ministers in mind. Yet or can be used by mental health professionals as well. These assessments help the user to understand the perspectives of the individual and use these to start the counseling process. The advantage of the spiritual assessments is they do not have an inherent bias. These assessments give a better understanding of the individual's perspectives and how to work with them on a better understanding of their faith and what this means to them. The spiritual assessments are used similarly to the other assessments covered yet use different questions to help start the introspection process.

The Faith Assessment starts off by asking, "What is faith to you?" This Key starts the conversation about their definition of faith. Now faith is not something that can easily be put into measurable terms, yet there are things that are tangential that can be put into measurable terms. An example of this is when an individual states they need to have a stronger faith. This can be tangentially measured by daily devotional time, more frequent church attendance, etc.

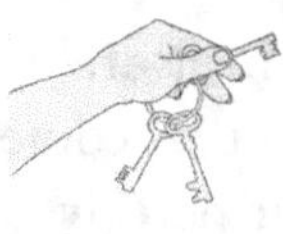

Faith Assessment

What is faith to you?	What do you want from your faith?	What is keeping you from growing in your faith?

The next Key is to collaborate with them to define faith in their own words. Work with the individual to get insight into any misconceptions and faulty information that might affect the client. Many individuals have "religious trauma" due to people who have manipulated religious teachings for their own purposes and warped individual's thoughts and feelings about faith. This assessment can help the individual to assess where their ideas about faith have come from.

The next Key is to collaborate with the individual to define the needs/wants in measurable terms. Then use the time line Key to help the individual develop timelines for these goals that come out of the needs/wants. The last Key is to collaborate with the individual to define their perceived barriers. The Key to using positivity is important for the collaboration with the individual to change the barriers listed in the responses to keep you from growing in your faith to how these can be overcome. Then collaborate with the individual to state these goals in measurable terms with timelines.

The Fellowship Assessments can be used when an individual is seeking a church or worship group to get involved with. The first Key is to have the individual define the goals they list as their needs/wants in measurable terms. The next Key is to collaborate with the individual on developing a timeline for their goals.

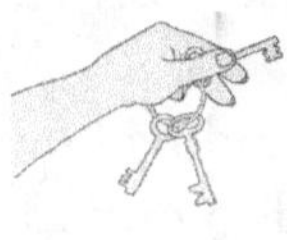

Fellowship Assessment

What do you need from a fellowship?	What do you want from a fellowship?	What are things that are standing in your way from being part of a fellowship?

Some of the responses and goals can be very specific or made specific, "I need a [fellowship] where I can get alcohol recovery help," "I need a fellowship that has programs for my kids," etc. The next Key to this assessment is to collaborate with what is standing their way from being a part of a fellowship. Collaborate with the individual on the last Key of developing positive ways they can overcome the barriers they list. The last step is assisting the individual one making these positives measurable to overcome the perceived barriers.

The Serving Others Assessments is a great tool to work with individuals in understanding how they can get involved in different ministries or groups to help others. The questions used to prompt the introspection are slightly different in this assessment.

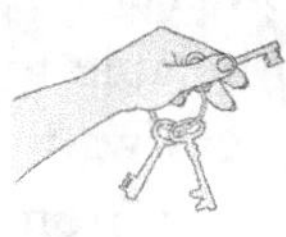

Serving Others Assessment

What do you need from serving others?	What do you want when you serve others?	What keeps you from getting involved in serving others?

The first Key asks, "What do you need to be able to serve others?" This question is worded to get them to start the introspection about their needs/wants from serving others. The next Key is to ask the individual to define what they list in needs/wants in measurable terms. Then they use the Key of setting timelines for achieving the goals listed in what they feel they need to get started to serve others. When asking clarification questions about what needs/wants from serving others, start to have them understand some of their strengths. It is important for the individual to be able to identify their strengths. The next Key is to collaborate with the individual to state the needs/wants of serving others in measurable terms. The Key question of "What is standing in your way from serving others?" is where the individual identifies obstacles for themselves. The Key to restructuring the perceived barriers into positives the individual can overcome is the last step.

CHAPTER 7

Health Care Needs Assessments

The health care needs assessments are designed to work with health professionals who do not have many assessments or are typically not trained to use assessments outside of their scope of practice. These assessments were designed to be used by dentists, physical therapists, and veterinarians. I had gotten feedback from people in these professions on some tools that would be beneficial for them. Often, dentists and veterinarians deal with other issues besides their field of expertise. These assessments are designed to be used in paper form or verbally, depending on the user's needs and preferences. It is important that these professionals have relationships with mental health professionals to be able to refer to when they feel the issues are more than they can handle.

Dental Needs Assessment

Let's face it. The dentist's office is not the first place that most people want to visit. This assessment can be used by dental offices to help reassure individuals and know how to overcome barriers the individual perceives to dental care. There are a lot of times that people get very anxious while visiting a dental office. This assessment can help the dental staff relieve the anxiety of the individual.

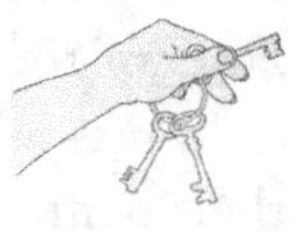

Dental Assessment

What do you need from dental care?	What do you want from dental care?	What is keeping you from getting dental care?

The Dental Assessment can help focus the individual on the care that they need. Many dentists get situations where individuals unload a lot of their other anxieties and fears when they are stressed about dental care. This assessment can help the individual remain focused on dental care without coming across as uncaring. The Dental Assessment can also help dental professionals understand what barriers individuals have to getting dental care. This assessment can be used verbally or have the individual complete before the office visit. The first Key is to focus on the needs/wants of the individual for their dental care. Collaborate with the individual to state their dental needs/wants in realistic and measurable terms. The last Key is to help the individual identify barriers to their dental care. This is an opportunity to work with the individual to overcome the perceived barriers. The last Key is to collaborate with the individual to reframe the barriers into positive ways to overcome the barriers they perceive as standing in their way of getting dental care.

Physical Therapy Assessment

The assessment that focuses on physical therapy was developed to help the physical therapist identify what can motivate the individual as well as perceived barriers individuals might have to overcome. Having worked with many physical therapists over my career, I have learned that progress is often determined as much by the individual's attitude and perception as by the exercises done. The Physical Therapy Assessment is designed to help the user understand what can motivate the individual and what is keeping them from getting the most from physical therapy.

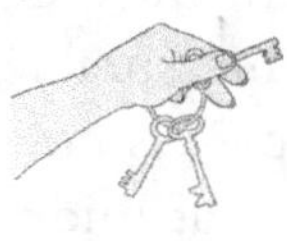

Physical Therapy Assessment

What do you need from physical therapy?	What do you want from physical therapy?	What is standing in your way from doing physical therapy?

The first Key question is, "What do you need from physical therapy?" This is where you can get an understanding if they know what to expect or if they have unrealistic expectations. If they are not able to give a response to this question, then explaining in more detail what physical therapy can do for them is a great place to start. The Key to what the individual wants from individual therapy can give insight into what can motivate the individual to work with the physical therapist. Using the clarification questions like, "How can we define the needs and wants for physical therapy in measurable terms?" The Key question of "What is standing in your way from doing physical therapy?" is how this assessment can help identify perceived barriers. Individuals can often have emotions or attitudes that are barriers to success with physical therapy. The last Key can assist the user in collaborating with the individual to develop positive ways to overcome the perceived barriers identified.

Veterinarian

Veterinarians are great, caring medical professionals for our dear nonhuman family members. Dealing with the owners of these nonhuman family members can be difficult at times. This assessment is slightly different as it focuses on what the pet needs rather than what the owner needs.

Veterinarian Assessment

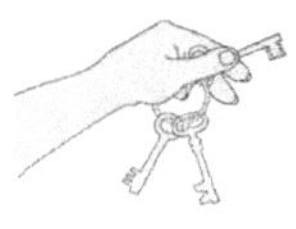

What do you need for your pet?	What do you want for your pet?	What is keeping you from getting the help/care your pet needs?

The purpose of this is to help veterinarians and veterinarian technicians to help focus on the needs of the pets. People get very attached to their pets, and often, these emotions can get focused on the ones attempting to take care of their pets. This assessment helps keep the individuals focused on the care of their pets. This can be especially helpful when there are hard quality or end-of-life choices being made. Veterinarians do their best to care for nonhuman family members and are often put into positions where they do not have the training to help the pet owners. This assessment can help the veterinarian focus on the needs of the pet and then guide the owner to resources to help them with the emotional turmoil the individual can have. There are many mental health resources to help an individual with grief or loss. Building a referral network is helpful for veterinarians so they can focus on what they do best and allow mental health professionals to assist them. The first Key is to ask the individual what they need/want for their pet. There are several things that can be identified as the individual answers the needs/wants that might indicate the individual needs a referral to mental health professionals.

Using this assessment can help when an owner focuses on alleviating the pain of the pet, this can be an indicator that the owner might be the one drug-seeking. When asking what the owner needs/wants for their pet, collaborate with the owner on what are reasonable and unreasonable expectations for their pet. The last Key is to ask what is standing in the way of the individual from getting the help that their pet needs. Collaborate with the individual to reframe the identified barriers into positives that can be overcome. This can include directing the individual to other resources that can help them to better care for their pets.

It is important to have a mental health therapist or agency to be able to refer individuals who need further assistance.

CHAPTER 8

Financial Assessments

The financial assessments are developed to be used by financial advisers as well as mental health professionals. There are other financial assessments that are used. The Key System Assessments differ in that these focus on the emotional perceptions of the individuals. The emotions of individuals or couples can affect their ability to achieve financial goals. These assessments are designed to help the user identify emotional aspects that can assist or stand in the way of the individual reaching financial goals. The financial assessments are geared to help individuals sort through the minefield of money and assets and start making short and long-term plans for themselves.

The first of these assessments is the Career Assessment. This can be used in two ways: First, if someone is just starting into or starting back into the workforce, focus on "job" and not "career." For the job, these are typically positions that people get that are a stepping stone to other long-term career jobs or just getting work experience and a paycheck. A career, in these terms, is focused on a type of work that the individual will be in for long periods. Now, in this job and career market, it is not unusual for people to change careers several times during their working lives.

Now working with the Career Assessment for a job, this can help the individual focus on what job or career will help them to reach the financial goals they have. The Career Assessment covered in the individual assessments section in this book focuses on the mental health aspects. For financial advisers, the focus can be on what jobs or career paths help the individual reach their goals financially and not as much on the mental health side. The focus is to help the individual on what career or jobs can help them to reach their long-term goals.

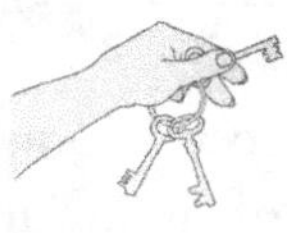

Career Assessment

What do you need in a job/career?	What do you want from a job/career?	What are things that you would not tolerate in a job/career?

The first Key is to ask the individual to define what they list as needs/wants in measurable terms so they can know when they are making progress toward financial goals. The Key here is how these needs/wants can be defined in a way to reach overall financial goals. The last Key to use is to have the individual identify barriers and how these perceived barriers can stand in their way to financial goals. When the individual lists things you would not tolerate in a job/career, work with them on how they can overcome these to be able to reach financial goals.

The Financial Assessment is a tool to use to assist individuals to use introspection to work on developing their financial goals. The first Key is to ask what the individual's definition of financial success is. The next Key is to ask the question, "What do you need from your financial resources?"

Financial Assessment

What do you need from your financial resources?	What do you want from your financial resources?	What is standing in the way of reaching your financial goals?

The first Key is to use clarification questions to help the individual put these needs in measurable terms. The next Key is to assist the individual in understanding if goals are obtainable and reasonable. The second question, "What do you want from your financial resources helps the individual make a distinction between needs and wants?" This assists the financial adviser in understanding the individual's priorities. This can assist the financial adviser in making a plan that will best serve the individual. There are situations where individuals need to make difficult choices to reach their financial needs/wants. This is a time to help the individual understand how they can prioritize their financial goals. The last Key of the assessment is asking, "What is standing in your way of reaching your financial goals?" This is where the individual identifies what they think are barriers to reaching their financial goals. Collaborating with the individual to find positive ways to overcome what is standing in their way is helpful. The development of obtainable financial goals to assist the individual in understanding they can overcome their perceived barriers. Collaborate with the individual on where they can start to reach their financial goals.

The financial assessment can also be used with couples as well. The use here is similar to what has been outlined in this chapter. The difference in using this assessment with couples is to have them both complete the assessment. The first Key is to ask each individual what their definition of financial success is. The next Key is to look at the similarities of the responses of each individual. Then focus on the individual responses that are different from each other. The next Key is to collaborate with the individuals to define these needs/wants in measurable and obtainable terms. This starts the discussion about priorities for their financial goals. The next Key is to have the couple list these goals in order of importance for them and then break down these goals into smaller steps to be able to gauge progress. The next Key is to work on the barriers that they think are standing in their way. Change the perceived barriers to their financial success into positives by focusing on how these can be overcome and how to measure progress.

The Retirement Assessment is designed to work with individuals and couples who are starting to work toward retirement. The first Key to use for individuals is to ask what their ideal is for living in retirement. The next Key starts by asking, "What do you need in retirement?" Start by asking the individual how they can make this measurable and/or obtainable with smaller steps to be able to reach these financial retirement goals.

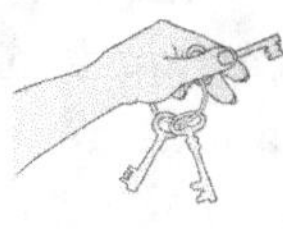

Retirement Assessment

What do you need when you retire?	What do you want from retirement?	What is keeping you from retirement?

The next Key question asked is "What do you want from retirement?" Ask the individual the clarification questions to help them to understand which of their wants are reasonable and/or obtainable is the next step. After the individual has defined their needs/wants in measurable terms, then work with them to prioritize these goals and the financial resources it will take to reach these goals. The Key question of "What is keeping you from retirement?" helps the individual to identify barriers. This last Key is changing these perceived obstacles into positives so that they can start to overcome their financial barriers to achieving their retirement goals. Lastly, a discussion about their wishes for the division of financial resources and other assets is an important discussion for the couple or individual. Work toward agreement on the division of the financial and other assets after they die.

When working with couples, the Keys used for the Retirement Assessment are similar to the Financial Assessment when working with couples. When the individual has unrealistic expectations for their financial resources, this is a good time to have a mental health therapist you can refer the individual to. When working with a couple and their goals are conflicting, and they are not able to have an agreement with a plan, this is a time to refer them to a trusted couples therapist to assist them.

CHAPTER 9

Coaching/Physical Training Assessments

This group of assessments was designed for those that work with a physical focus. These assessments are focused on where individuals are involved in physical activities like sports or working out. The mindset of an individual can be helpful and motivating or can keep them from reaching their full potential. When there are psychological barriers to their physical goals, this can keep the individual from achieving the goals they want. When an individual is playing sports, they can have psychological barriers that can affect their performance and motivation. When a person is participating in physical training, the emotional state can assist or stand in the way of the individual getting the most out of physical training. Individuals go to gyms and physical trainers to reach the goals they have. Psychological attitudes can help or hinder an individual's long-term commitment to physical training. These assessments can help identify potential attitudes that can be helpful or barriers to individuals.

The Workout Assessment can help the user to understand the mindset of an individual regarding their needs, wants, and what is standing in the way for them when it comes to working out.

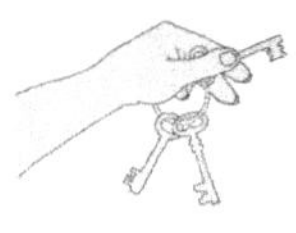

Workout Assessment

What do you need from working out?	What do you want from working out?	What is standing in your way from working out?

Individuals can have a lot of expectations that may not be realistic in what they can achieve or the time frame to get the results they are looking for when working out. Motivation is Key to helping people achieve their workout goals. The Workout Assessment can help identify what can be used to help motivate individuals. A Key is to work through what the individual needs/wants from working out. Specifically, what an individual lists in their wants can help them identify what can be used to motivate the individual. Both the needs and wants help the individual to start and keep up with the workout routines. The Workout Assessment can, more importantly, help identify what is standing in the way of motivation.

This assessment can be used as a form or as questions that the user writes down the responses. The starting point is to have the individual define his needs/wants in measurable terms with time lines. This is a good time to understand if the individual has realistic or unrealistic goals for their workout goals. Now the user can work with the individual to have realistic goals and timelines for their workout routines.

The last Key is the column that asks, "What is standing in your way from working out?" The responses can give insight into what the individual believes are barriers for the individual. The last Key is changing the barriers into positives that can overcome the negative barriers. With the barriers identified, the user can help focus on the potential that they can achieve. There is a possibility that there are deeper issues that might come to light during this assessment. This is a time to refer the individual to mental health therapy.

Most coaches I have known and worked with have told me that mental attitude and perception are extremely important for the athlete's success. The Sports Assessment is a tool to help coaches understand the individual athlete and what motivates them to improve. The first Key asks, "What do you need from sport?" The sport can be written in since the Sports Assessment can be used for almost any sport. The sport is filled in to be specific, like football, volleyball, basketball, or any given sport. The next question is, "What do you want from sport?"

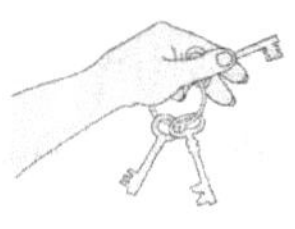

Sports Assessment

What do you need from _____________?	What do you want from _____________?	What is standing in your way from doing your best in _____________?

This Key can give an insight into what the athlete needs/wants from participating in that sport. Getting the needs/wants into measurable terms can then help the individual use these to increase their motivation. The last Key asks, "What is standing in your way from doing your best in sport?" Taking what the individual lists here and collaborating with them on what can counter what they have listed as barriers. The last Key is to focus on how the barriers can be overcome in a measurable way.

There are responses that might need a referral for mental health therapy. Some examples of responses that would be appropriate for a referral are as follows: "I need to play to be popular," "I need to play so I don't get picked on," "I need to play to please a family member." Statements like these can indicate that there are other underlying issues that counseling should be used to help them overcome to reach their full potential. Another referral could come from someone who is using sports to achieve fame. An individual who is primarily wanting to be in sports to achieve fame has potential issues that can be counter to team sports. These individuals need help to learn that competition is a team effort and not just for them.

CHAPTER 10

Teaching Music/Tutoring

The teaching assessments are designed for private music teachers and academic tutors. There are not many assessments that music teachers or academic tutors can use. These assessments are designed to assist music teachers and academic tutors in identifying psychological motivators and barriers. The barriers can keep an individual from reaching their goals. The Key Assessments can be used to identify potential barriers. Working to change the barriers into positives can assist the individual in reaching learning goals.

There are a lot of people who teach music, and the Musical Needs Assessment can help them identify the barriers individuals have toward learning music. The first Key is the question of, What do you need/want from learning music? This helps the user to understand what motivates the individual.

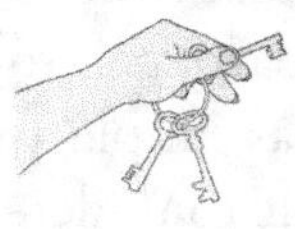

Music Learning Assessment

What do you need from learning to play music?	What do you want from learning music?	What is standing in your way from learning to plan music?

When asking what an individual needs from learning music, look for realistic or unrealistic goals. If the individual has unrealistic ideas, then help them to understand what realistic goals would be and how to measure progress toward this. Often, music students want instantaneous learning and this is a time to help them understand the learning process and realistic time lines. The next Key is asking about what is standing in the way of the individual learning music. This is a great time to understand what barriers they have. The last Key is to question about how to turn these barriers into positives and how to overcome the obstacles they feel they have. These obstacles can be as simple as not having a routine for practice, a place to practice, the correct instrument, not being able to understand how to read music or any number of obstacles the individual identifies. Ask how the individual can define some ways they can work toward overcoming their obstacles. Work with the individual on reframing these identified obstacles into positives that can overcome the obstacles. The last Key is to assist the individual to know how they can measure their progress in overcoming the obstacles.

People who tutor individuals in most educational environments can use the Tutoring Needs Assessment in a way to help identify what motivates the individual and barriers individuals have toward learning certain subjects. These assessments can be used to help identify barriers that individuals have toward learning.

Tutoring Assessment

What do you need from tutoring?	What do you want from tutoring?	What is keeping you from learning?

The first Key is asking what the individual needs/wants from tutoring. This Key will give insight into what the tutor can focus on to help the individual motivate themselves to study. Individuals seek out tutoring for many reasons. Understanding the reason for seeking out tutoring can assist the tutor in finding what can motivate the individual. Tutors often spend a lot of time initially finding out where to start the tutoring process. This assessment can help the tutor know where they can start working with the individual. The Tutoring Assessment can also help the tutor know where the individual feels they need to start. When going over the needs/wants the individual has listed, it is important to go over realistic and unrealistic expectations the individual might have for tutoring. The next step is to use the clarification questions to help the individual define these needs/wants in measurable terms so they can know their progress.

As with all these assessments, the Key of "What is keeping you from learning?" is important for the individual to list their barriers. After the individual has identified barriers that are impeding their learning process, then the user should collaborate with the individual on reframing these barriers into positives. Work with the individuals on how they can measure progress in overcoming their barriers. This can help a tutor address potential emotional barriers that can stand in the way of the individual learning the material.

CHAPTER 11

The Final Key

The Key System of Informal Assessments was designed initially as an intake assessment to help develop treatment plans. After using this intake assessment, the versatility of this design became evident, and the development of other assessments began. These assessments have been used in various forms for many years of my therapy practice. There have been a few therapists and others in mental health who have used early versions of these assessments and encouraged me to share these on a larger scale. The assessments were shared with my friend and minister, Dr. Wade Bibb, and after he started using these, it encouraged me to write this book and share these assessments. The Key System of Informal Assessments has been copyrighted and is free to anyone who possesses a copy of this book. The assessments described in this book are intended to give another tool for those in helping professions to use. These assessments are designed to be flexible and effective. Using the introspection of the individuals is a process to start therapeutic relationships. The strength of an informal assessment over more formal assessments is the responses are directly from the perspective of the individual. These informal assessments are not intended to replace formal assessments. These assessments have the ability to be applied and used by many other professions besides those that are in mental health. The simplicity of these assessments makes them where they are able to be used with simple training and understanding. The ideas for these assessments and this book, I believe, have come from my faith in God Almighty guiding me.

ABOUT THE AUTHOR

G. Lamont Douglas lives with his wife, Kristi, in Knoxville, Tennessee, where he is a Licensed Professional Counselor in private practice. His daughter (Evelynn Douglas) designed the artwork for this book, assessments, and website. Lamont attended the University of Tennessee for both his bachelor's in psychology and master's in community agency counseling with a minor in marriage and family counseling. He has been a mental health therapist for over twenty-five years and has worked in multiple mental health roles over the course of his career. Lamont grew up as a preacher's kid and has been active in churches all of his life and continues to play in his church orchestra. He enjoys cooking and entertaining family and friends with his wife, Kristi. Lamont can often be found working with his hands on projects around his home and with friends. His favorite outdoor activities are bicycling and kayaking when he can find the time. Lamont and his wife Kristi are big Disney fans and share this interest with several longtime friends.